Bible
Word Search
Collection #2

Compiled and Edited by
Carol Borror Leath

A Barbour Book

Bible Word Search Collection #2
© MCMXCVI by Barbour & Company, Inc.

ISBN 1-55748-882-7

All Scripture quotations marked (KJV) are taken from
The Authorized King James Version of the Bible.

Scripture quotations marked (RSV) are from the Revised
Standard Version of the Bible, copyright 1946, 1952, 1971 by
the Division of Christian Education of the National Council
of the Church of Christ in the USA. Used by permission.

Published by Barbour & Company, Inc.
              P.O. Box 719
              Uhrichsville, OH 44683
              e-mail: books<barbour@tusco.net>

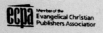
Member of the
Evangelical Christian
Publishers Association

Printed in the United States of America.

Bible
Word Search
Collection #2

Word Search 1

FOR WHAT SIN SHALL NO MAN
BE FORGIVEN?

Locate and loop only the words underlined in this verse found in Luke 12:10 (KJV).

"And whosoever shall speak a word against the Son of man, it shall be forgiven him: but unto him that blasphemeth against the Holy Ghost it shall not be forgiven."

BONUS BIBLE TRIVIA

People weren't given permission to eat meat until after the flood. Genesis 9:3

B	F	E	S	P	E	A	K	I	D	H
H	S	O	N	O	F	M	A	N	T	O
F	L	J	R	N	G	M	K	E	C	L
U	O	V	E	G	X	Q	M	U	S	Y
R	N	T	V	W	I	E	Y	H	P	G
A	S	T	E	C	H	V	G	I	Z	H
F	H	D	O	P	B	H	E	M	E	O
L	A	I	S	O	S	M	Q	N	K	S
J	L	A	O	A	G	A	I	N	S	T
P	L	N	H	V	T	X	R	D	B	E
B	U	Z	W	O	R	D	A	C	W	Y

Word Search 2

GOD TESTS ABRAHAM

Read all about Abraham and his son Isaac and what happened when they went to the land of Moriah in Genesis 22:1-19.

ABRAHAM	MULTIPLY
ANGEL	NATIONS
BLESS	OBEYED
BOUND ISAAC	OFFER
BUILT ALTAR	POSSESS
BURNT OFFERING	RAM
CUT WOOD	ROSE EARLY
DESCENDANTS	SECOND TIME
ENEMIES	SLAY
FEAR GOD	SON
FIRE	SWORN
GATE	TESTED
HAND	"THE LORD WILL PROVIDE"
HORNS	THICKET
KNIFE	THIRD DAY
LAND OF MORIAH	TWO YOUNG MEN
LIFTED UP EYES	"WHERE IS THE LAMB?"
LOVE	WORSHIP
MOUNTAIN	

```
E S T N A D N E C S E D A F N Y C O
M D O O W T U C D E H D O G R A E F
I L I F T E D U P E Y E S B O D G F
T I F V X L O N O S Q Y T A W D A E
D P I R O S J W K N I F E B S R M R
N C R K V R Z N S U R B M R C I L D
O A E L G E P S J A K A G A Y H A P
C A H A N G E L T F L N A H L T N S
E S B I R S M L L E O R T A P H D Q
S I T L S O A X H I A W E M I A O C
V D Y O E T S T U Z W V B M T N F D
P N P E L S S E I G O D K A L D M T
I U H I F I S J E L M L R R U E O E
H O U N E O P N I A T N U O M T R K
S B U R N T O F F E R I N G L S I C
R S E I M E N E Q Y A L S U S E A I
O H O R N S R V T O B E Y E D T H H
W S N O I T A N E M G N U O Y O W T
```

Word Search 3

GOOD SAMARITAN

Find out what happened to the man who "fell among robbers" in Luke 10:29-37.

BEAT	ONE WHO SHOWED MERCY
BOUND UP WOUNDS	PASSED BY ON OTHER SIDE
BROUGHT TO INN	POURED ON OIL AND WINE
COMPASSION	PRIEST
FELL AMONG ROBBERS	PROVED NEIGHBOR
INNKEEPER	SAMARITAN
JERICHO	SET ON OWN BEAST
JERUSALEM	STRIPPED
LEVITE	TWO DENARII

BONUS BIBLE TRIVIA

Locusts, katydids, crickets, and grasshoppers were considered clean food for the Israelites. What's for lunch? Leviticus 11:22

```
P O U R E D O N O I L A N D W I N E B
N A T I R A M A S C K G V O T E M I Q
F L S F J D H N N I O T T H G U O R B
E N I S W R A G S E P C U Y J K H D C
L X I R E P E E K N N I B F Z I D E L
L O R L S D X N B V D Q F Y K H A P B
A P A M R O B H G I E N D E V O R P O
M T N C E G R Y J W L U I Z O R M I U
O N E W H O S H O W E D M E R C Y R N
N S D N U P A Q Y N C N E K W J M T D
G X O B Z F I T D G O V L H P O N S U
R G W Q A W N I C I S T Y K E P U L P
O V T H M B R X S O J D H T Z R F P W
B U Q J E R U S A L E M J E R I C H O
B F V Y R W A H O A J E L S R E R C U
E N G T X P I T Z P K B Q T D S M S N
R B A E M I G P L N D J H Q O T I N D
S E T O N O W N B E A S T C K F M D S
B V C R B U D A E C S R T L E V I T E
```

Word Search 4

ISAAC AND REBEKAH

Find out how and why Rebekah was chosen to be the wife of Isaac in Genesis 24.

ABRAHAM

AROSE IN THE MORNING

BLESSED IN ALL THINGS

BORN TO BETHUEL

BROTHER LABAN

CHOICE GIFTS

CITY OF NAHOR

COSTLY ORNAMENTS

COVERED HERSELF

DEPARTED

DRINK

FATHER'S HOUSE

FOOD

GOLD RING

HE LOVED HER

ISAAC

JAR

LIFTED UP EYES

LODGE

MAIDEN

MEDITATE IN THE FIELD

MESOPOTAMIA

RAIMENT

REBEKAH

SERVANT

SHOULDER

SILVER AND GOLD

SPENT THE NIGHT

SPRING

STEDFAST LOVE

TAKE A WIFE

TEN CAMELS

TENT

TIME OF EVENING

TROUGH

TWO BRACELETS

VEIL

VERY FAIR

VIRGIN

WATER CAMELS

WELL OF WATER

```
M T N A V R E S P E N T T H E N I G H T
S E Y E P U D E T F I L O D G E B E G I
D F D A C E E V O L T S A F D E T S U M
C H O I C E G I F T S S P R I N G T O E
J G I M T A K E A W I F E N R N O N R O
A J N A E A H R E B E K A H I K L E T F
R B E T N R T L S P R B O H A S D M R E
E O D O C A M E Q T A N T I F H R A E V
S R I P A I C S I L E L V S Y O I N T E
U N A O M M U I R N L L T A R U N R A N
O T M S E E W E T A T N E A E L G O W I
H O A E L N H X N Y Z H I C V D A Y F N
S B H M S T L I E V O Y E G A E B L O G
R E A F O O D C F H J F E F R R G T L I
E T R R D E P A R T E D N D I I B S L T
H H B K S L E M A C R E T A W E V O E N
T U A S L R E H D E V O L E H N L C W E
A E E P O S I L V E R A N D G O L D M T
F L E S R E H D E R E V O C Q D R I N K
B G N I N R O M E H T N I E S O R A S R
```

11

Word Search 5

JACOB'S TWELVE SONS

ASHER

BENJAMIN

DAN

GAD

ISSACHAR

JOSEPH

JUDAH

LEVI

NAPHTALI

REUBEN

SIMEON

ZEBULUN

BONUS BIBLE TRIVIA

King Ahab disguised himself in a battle so the enemy wouldn't try to kill him, but a random arrow hit him anyway. 1 Kings 22:29-35

```
S   I   M   E   O   N   L   P   J
R   A   H   C   A   S   S   I   O
Z   E   Q   J   T   N   L   V   S
E   R   U   I   U   A   B   R   E
B   Z   V   B   T   D   E   U   P
U   E   W   H   E   H   A   C   H
L   S   P   X   S   N   G   H   O
U   A   M   A   D   A   N   A   Y
N   I   M   A   J   N   E   B   D
```

Word Search 6

JESUS IN THE TEMPLE

Find out what Jesus said to his mother and father when they found him in the temple in Luke 2:43-52.

AMAZED   QUESTIONS

ANSWERS   STATURE

ASTONISHED   SUBJECT

DOCTORS   TARRIED

"FATHER'S BUSINESS"   TEMPLE

HEARING   THREE DAYS

JERUSALEM   TWELVE YEARS OLD

JESUS   UNDERSTANDING

JOSEPH   WISDOM

MOTHER

NAZARETH

BONUS BIBLE TRIVIA

The disciples were first called Christians in Antioch. Acts 11:26

```
F C E K A S T O N I S H E D J
G A L I Q P S M T E M P L E F
N M T C E J B U S D R O H G O
T A Y H P E S O J A S V N N B
W Z A J E S U S U R Y I C I Z
S E S N X R A D A F D M M R C
Y D T B S E S E G N H O E A Q
A I A M P W Y B A K T D L E U
D N T O J E E T U H L S A H E
E Q U T V Z S R E S U I S W S
E S R L X R V R S R I W U Y T
R A E D E I R R A T C N R E I
H W F D B N R D J G V P E L O
T H N A Z A R E T H W U J S N
Q U O K T M S I D O C T O R S
```

Word Search 7

JESUS' UNANSWERABLE QUESTION

Locate and loop only the words underlined in these verses found in Matthew 22:41-46 (KJV).

"While the <u>Pharisees</u> were <u>gathered</u> <u>together</u>, Jesus <u>asked</u> them, <u>Saying</u>, What <u>think</u> ye of <u>Christ</u>? whose <u>son</u> is he?

They say <u>unto</u> him, The son of <u>David</u>.

He <u>saith</u> unto them, How then doth David in <u>spirit</u> call him <u>Lord</u>, saying, The Lord <u>said</u> unto my Lord, <u>Sit</u> thou on my <u>right hand</u>, till I <u>make</u> thine <u>enemies</u> thy <u>footstool</u>? If David then <u>call</u> him Lord, how is he his son?

And <u>no man</u> was <u>able</u> to <u>answer</u> him a <u>word</u>, <u>neither</u> <u>durst</u> any man from that day <u>forth</u> ask him any more <u>questions</u>."

```
I S T L G A T H E R E D N
H T I A S O M G N I Y A S
T P S K R E H T E G O T R
R T E A B L E Q T H I N K
O D Q S F O O T S T O O L
F U S U A R N E Z H C W L
X B O S E D E V S A I D A
N T N E Y S I E D N T R C
O S F J I J T V L D I O I
M I M R K M H I A G R W U
A R A N S W E R O D I H N
N H K O T S R U D N P N T
P C E P E N E M I E S Q O
```

Word Search 8

JEZEBEL

Who was Naboth and why was he stoned to death?
Find out in 1 Kings 21.

AHAB

BLOOD

CHARGE

DOGS

EAT NO FOOD

ELDERS

ELIJAH

EVIL

FASTED

HUMBLED

JEZEBEL

KING OF SAMARIA

NABOTH

NOBLES

PALACE

RENT CLOTHES

SACKCLOTH

SHE WROTE LETTERS

STONE TO DEATH

SULLEN

TAKE POSSESSION

"THE LORD FORBID"

TWO BASE FELLOWS

VALUE IN MONEY

VEGETABLE GARDEN

VEXED

VINEYARD

```
V T H E L O R D F O R B I D A G D
K E C A L A P E H C D K Y F J S I
I B G L N B L E B E Z E J R R T M
N D N E Q A A D T Y N O Z E T O B
G S O P T H W S E O R V T N X N J
O D B O C A A E M X H T A T F E R
F R L H F F B N B G E I D C J T A
S A E A K O I L N L P V O L Q O S
A Y S J M E N N E L L U S O L D K
M E R I U W Z T V G T E S T H E J
A N U L X A O Y A S A G G H T A D
R I A E S R E D L E B R O E O T E
I V C F W B L O O D G A D S B H L
A E I E V I L M O H J H K E A D B
L P H T O L C K C A S C N R N Q M
U S W O L L E F E S A B O W T S U
T A K E P O S S E S S I O N V T H
```

Word Search 9

JOB

What did Job do when he found out his sons and daughters had been killed? Find out in Job 1-42.

APPOINTMENT

BILDAD

BLAMELESS

BLESSED LATTER DAYS

BULLS

BURNT OFFERINGS

CAMELS

CHALDEANS

ELIHU BECAME ANGRY

ELIPHAZ

FEARED GOD

GREAT WIND

LAND OF UZ

LOATHSOME SORES

MESSENGER TO JOB

MONEY

OXEN

PRAYED FOR FRIENDS

RAMS

RENT HIS ROBE

RESTORED FORTUNES

RING OF GOLD

SABEANS

SATAN

SERVANTS

SEVEN SONS

SHAVED HIS HEAD

SHEEP

SLEW

STRUCK HOUSE

SUFFERING

THREE DAUGHTERS

THREE FRIENDS

UPRIGHT

WORSHIPED

YOUNG PEOPLE DEAD

ZOPHAR

```
B E L I H U B E C A M E A N G R Y B E L
Y L R E N T H I S R O B E C F Y E N O M
O H E D G H I D A E H S I H D E V A H S
U N P S L R A P P O I N T M E N T J L M
N M E S S E N G E R T O J O B H K S A S
G R O G E E B L A M E L E S S G T N N D
P Q R N V D D E P I H S R O W R H A D N
E X S I E A Z L C U T A M W U E R E O E
O D Y R N U S T A N B E V C P A E D F I
P E L E S G I A A T S F K H R T E L U R
L J K F O H O V B O T H G A I W F A Z F
E Q M F N T R F R E O E H O G I R H A R
D P R U S E N E G U A P R S H N I C H O
E C T S S R S V S O O N W D T D E A P F
A R B E U S D E Y Z L A S X A Z N M I D
D A D L I B F E A R E D G O D Y D E L E
F M C B U R N T O F F E R I N G S L E Y
H S G K J S H E E P D I L E W E L S M A
Q S L L U B N R X U S A T A N P X T V R
R E S T O R E D F O R T U N E S O S W P
```

Word Search 10

JOHN 3:16

This verse has been translated into over 1100 languages. Find 25 of them in the puzzle.

AFRIKAANS	ITALIAN
ARABIC	JAPANESE
CHINESE	KOREAN
DANISH	MALAY
DUTCH	NORWEGIAN
ENGLISH	PORTUGUESE
FINNISH	RUSSIAN
FRENCH	SINHALESE
GERMAN	SPANISH
GREEK	SWEDISH
HEBREW	TAMIL
HINDI	VIETNAMESE
ICELANDIC	

```
V A F R I K A A N S L A O C K
U I Q V N A Y H I N D I S I O
D P E T E S E N A P A J M B R
B A W T F Z H E H K H X C A E
M N N G N A J S M D L I F R A
R A O I L A I E U E H Q I A N
T M L E S D M H S P S V N S C
H R S A E H C E W E I A N Y I
S E V W Y N U Z S B N L I D D
I G S X E G F C H E A I S U N
L I D R U S S I A N P M H T A
G K F T L E O N G J S A M C L
N O R W E G I A N P W T R H E
E O U Q Z X W E R B E H Y S C
P V G R E E K T N A I L A T I
```

Word Search 11

JOHN THE BAPTIST

Read all about the birth, life, and death of John the Baptist and why a woman named Herodias held a grudge against him and wanted him beheaded in Matthew 3, Matthew 14:1-12, Mark 6:14-29, Luke 1:5-80, and Luke 3:1-20.

ANGEL
BANQUET
BAPTISM
BAPTIZED JESUS
BEHEADED
BIRTH
ELIZABETH
FORGIVENESS OF SINS
GARMENT OF CAMEL HAIR
GREW
GRUDGE
HERODIAS DANCED
HEROD'S BIRTHDAY
ISRAEL
JOHN
LEATHER GIRDLE

LOCUSTS
MANIFESTATIONS
MULTITUDES
PHARISEES
PLATTER
PREACHING GOOD NEWS
PRISON
REPENTANCE
RIVER JORDAN
SADDUCEES
SON
STRONG IN SPIRIT
WATER
WILDERNESS
WILD HONEY
ZECHARIAH

```
S T R O N G I N S P I R I T C W S R
N S E E C U D D A S E L E A R S I E
I A W G Y E L D R I G R E H T A E L
S U S E J D E Z I T P A B I H Y U I
F S H S N F O K L J D L B L A A Y Z
O N W I L D H O N E Y Q E M I D U A
S O I W N H O J O H G M H W R H N B
S I L N A Q X O T D A N E B A T A E
E T D E G D U R G C E R A V H R D T
N A E P T M I P F G G I D S C I R H
E T R G K B C O E R N N E T E B O Z
V S N R E T T A L P S I D S Z S J L
I E E B A N Q U E T O J H U Z D R N
G F S R E T A W X T N B H C V O E O
R I S M U L T I T U D E S O A R V S
O N R E P E N T A N C E F L R E I I
F A D E C N A D S A I D O R E H R R
G M S I T P A B D S E E S I R A H P
```

Word Search 12

JONAH AND THE WHALE

Find out how Jonah found himself in the belly of a whale in Jonah 1-2.

BELLY	OFFERED SACRIFICE
CAPTAIN	PAID FARE
CAST LOTS	PRAYED
DRY LAND	PRESENCE OF LORD
FAST ASLEEP	SON OF AMITTAI
FISH	SWALLOW
GREAT WIND	TARSHISH
INNER PART OF SHIP	THREE DAYS AND NIGHTS
JOPPA	THREW JONAH INTO SEA
MADE VOWS	THREW WARES INTO SEA
MARINERS AFRAID	VOMITED
MIGHTY TEMPEST	WENT ON BOARD
NINEVEH	WICKEDNESS

```
O A D R O L F O E C N E S E R P C S
A F A S T A S L E E P D F B P I T O
E I F E M K G S T O L T S A C H S N
S S S E N D E K C I W H I D G S E O
O W J G R E A T W I N D D I L F P F
T O N W Q E V A F X F T N A P O M A
N V W R A O D I B A S D A R U T E M
I E E Y L B S S R C N A L F E R T I
S D N C B H D E A A D Z Y A N A Y T
E A T V M F I F S C H L R S I P T T
R M O O C J M Y E G R K D R A R H A
A P N M N O A P P O J I Q E T E G I
W N B I E D R T X V G S F N P N I D
W U O T E H E V E N I N W I A N M E
E Y A E S W A L L O W A H R C I C Y
R B R D P B E L L Y I P J A R E Z A
H H D E H S I H S R A T D M K G F R
T H R E W J O N A H I N T O S E A P
```

Word Search 13

LAST SUPPER

Find out what happened in the "upper room" in Luke 22:1-38.

APOSTLES	JUDAS ISCARIOT
BETRAY	LAMB
BLOOD	MONEY
BREAD	OFFICERS
CONFERRED	PASSOVER
COVENANT	PETER
CUP	PREPARE
DEATH	PRIESTS
DISCIPLES	REMEMBRANCE
DIVIDE	SACRIFICED
DRINK	SATAN
FEAST	SCRIBES
FRUIT OF THE VINE	TABLE
JESUS	UNLEAVENED BREAD
JOHN	UPPER ROOM
	WOE

```
U N L E A V E N E D B R E A D
P D D T C O N F E R R E D F E
P R R S E N N O G I R J T D C
E E I A B M A L F E H O Y E I
R T N E D T T R V F I H A R F
R E K F S I A O B R I N R A I
O P U C J T S B A M L C T P R
O J E S U S S C L N E K E E C
M B R E A D S M I E O M B R A
D Y Y P V I P U R P W S E P S
E I Q E S A P O S T L E S R T
A V V A N B Y T N A N E V O C
T D D I X O S E B I R C S C Z
H U E G D I M D H F B L O O D
J N N I V E H T F O T I U R F
```

Word Search 14

LONGEST VERSE IN THE BIBLE

Locate and loop only the words underlined in this verse found in Esther 8:9 (KJV).

"Then were the <u>king's</u> <u>scribes</u> <u>called</u> at that <u>time</u> in the <u>third</u> <u>month</u>, that is, the month <u>Sivan</u>, on the <u>three</u> and <u>twentieth</u> <u>day</u> <u>thereof</u>; and it was <u>written</u> <u>according</u> to all that <u>Mordecai</u> <u>commanded</u> unto the <u>Jews</u>, and to the <u>lieutenants</u>, and the <u>deputies</u> and <u>rulers</u> of the <u>provinces</u> which are from <u>India</u> unto <u>Ethiopia</u>, an <u>hundred</u> <u>twenty</u> and <u>seven</u> provinces, unto every province according to the <u>writing</u> thereof, and unto every <u>people</u> after their <u>language</u>, and to the Jews according to their writing, and according to their language."

```
T H E R E O F N T Q T H I R D
H P U A W R Y S R E L U R O A
R V S C R I B E S H T N O M Y
E S E C N I V O R P S D K X Z
E A F O O E K H C J S R I D E
D I G R L M W R I T T E N E B
O A I D N I M Q N S O D G P T
P E R I Y T C A L L E D S U W
N T X N B M N Z N E V E S T G
Y H A G T E M O R D E C A I N
C I H F T W E N T I E T H E I
G O K U I D E N J P L D E S T
M P E O P L E N A V I S W Q I
T I O W R A E Y T U D E Z C R
L A N G U A G E S Y J X V B W
```

Word Search 15

Locate and loop only the words underlined in these verses found in Matthew 6:9-13 (KJV).

"Our <u>Father</u> which <u>art</u> in <u>heaven</u>, <u>Hallowed</u> be thy <u>name</u>. Thy <u>kingdom</u> come. Thy <u>will</u> be <u>done</u> in <u>earth</u>, as it is in heaven.
<u>Give</u> us this <u>day</u> our <u>daily</u> <u>bread</u>.
And <u>forgive</u> us our <u>debts</u>, as we forgive our <u>debtors</u>.
And <u>lead</u> us not into <u>temptation</u>, but <u>deliver</u> us from <u>evil</u>:
For <u>thine</u> is the kingdom, and the <u>power</u>, and the <u>glory</u>, <u>for ever</u>. <u>Amen</u>."

BONUS BIBLE TRIVIA

Job's wife thought he had bad breath. Job 19:17

R	E	V	I	L	E	D	C	A	R	T
D	E	B	T	O	R	S	H	K	E	H
A	A	W	Y	R	O	L	G	M	V	I
M	R	E	O	E	D	S	P	O	E	N
E	T	V	V	P	D	T	E	D	R	E
N	H	I	F	A	A	B	V	G	O	I
E	G	G	E	T	I	E	I	N	F	L
V	E	R	I	J	L	D	L	I	N	W
A	B	O	D	A	Y	G	O	K	A	I
E	N	F	A	T	H	E	R	N	M	L
H	A	L	L	O	W	E	D	A	E	L

Word Search 16

MAJOR AND MINOR PROPHETS
(in the order they appear in the Bible)

ISAIAH	JONAH
JEREMIAH	MICAH
LAMENTATIONS	NAHUM
EZEKIEL	HABAKKUK
DANIEL	ZEPHANIAH
HOSEA	HAGGAI
JOEL	ZECHARIAH
AMOS	MALACHI
OBADIAH	

BONUS BIBLE TRIVIA

Israelites weren't allowed to eat camels. What a
sacrifice! Well, actually they weren't allowed to
sacrifice them either. Leviticus 11:4

```
Z E C H A R I A H L O S
N Q S E I A G G A H N P
A M O S Z V T E C O M R
W A I Y E E S C I U X J
B Z H D P O K T M F E O
E O C J H G A I N R I E
D B A L A T H K E M O L
A A L P N U O M W L N R
N D A E I Q I S A I A H
I I M X A A T A C V H Y
E A Z B H A B A K K U K
L H A N O J E L Q P M D
```

Word Search 17

MIRACLES OF THE LORD

(blind) BARTIMAEUS

(blind man at) BETHESDA

BLIND MAN

(miraculous) CATCH OF FISH

(Syrophenician's) DAUGHTER

DEAF, SPEECHLESS (man)

DEMON-POSSESSED (man)

(man with) DROPSY

EPILEPTIC BOY

FEEDING (of 5,000 people)

(wild man of) GADARA

(woman with) HEMORRHAGE

INFIRM WOMAN

(raising of) JAIRUS'

  DAUGHTER

(two blind men at) JERICHO

LAME MAN (at Bethesda)

(raising of) LAZARUS

(healing of) LEPER

MALCHUS' EAR

(Peter's) MOTHER-IN-LAW

NOBLEMAN'S SON

PALSIED MAN

(feeding of 4,000) PEOPLE

(walking on the) SEA

(Roman centurion's) SERVANT

(calming of the) STORM

TEN LEPERS

TWO BLIND MEN

(man with) UNCLEAN SPIRIT

(raising of) WIDOW'S SON

(water turned to) WINE

(man with) WITHERED HAND

```
J N O B L E M A N S S O N J B A W M
C A T C H O F F I S H B D E L W I R
E P I L E P T I C B O Y R R I I T O
C A N R L G M J E O R E O I N N H T
I L F H U D N L B A K F P C D E E S
U S I S P S P U E A W R S H M X R S
N I R R T O D S V Q R S Y O A S E E
C E M E E Y U A E A N T R C N E D L
L D W P Z H D G U E B R I F A A H H
E M O E C W N H M G H I O M R K A C
A A M L G I I D J A H L N P A M N E
N N A N D Q N D G U S T V T D E D E
S M N E R I W E O N A M E M A L U P
P X E T L E P E R W Z B D R G C A S
I F Y B T N A V R E S U R A Z A L F
R E O R E T H G U A D S E H T E B A
I W A L N I R E H T O M O G J L H E
T F K I D E S S E S S O P N O M E D
```

Word Search 18

MOST PRECIOUS VERSE

Locate and loop only the words underlined in this verse found in John 3:16 (KJV).

"For God so loved the world, that he gave his
only begotten son, that whosoever believeth in
him should not perish, but have everlasting life."

BONUS BIBLE TRIVIA

Nahor, Abraham's grandfather's name, means "snorer."

P	W	O	R	L	D	S	E	V	A	G
O	T	H	X	Q	A	N	Y	U	N	O
N	B	T	O	V	O	Z	W	I	R	D
L	F	E	B	S	J	G	T	E	K	E
Y	C	V	G	H	O	S	D	L	I	V
R	M	E	P	O	A	E	T	O	U	O
P	S	I	E	L	T	N	V	W	Q	L
L	X	L	R	V	B	T	D	E	F	A
I	C	E	I	E	Y	G	E	Z	R	H
F	V	B	S	I	M	L	O	N	P	K
E	J	S	H	O	U	L	D	N	O	T

Word Search 19

NAOMI AND RUTH

Find out what happened to Naomi and her daughter-in-law Ruth, and why Ruth was called a "woman of worth" in Ruth 1-4.

ANOINT
BARLEY HARVEST
BEST CLOTHES
BETHLEHEM
BOAZ TOOK RUTH
BORE SON
CHILION
CONCEPTION
DAUGHTERS-IN-LAW
ELIMELECH
EXCHANGING
FAMINE
FOUND FAVOR
GLEANED IN FIELD
GRACIOUS
HUSBAND DIED
JUDAH
KISSED
MAHLON
MAN OF WEALTH
MARA
MEALTIME
MIDNIGHT

MOAB
MORNING
NAOMI
NURSE
OBED
ORPAH
REDEEMING
RUTH CLUNG TO HER
SANDAL
SHEAVES
SIX MEASURES
SONS DIED
SONS TOOK WIVES
STARTLED
TEN YEARS
THRESHING FLOOR
TOWN WAS STIRRED
TWO SONS
UNCOVERED HIS FEET
WASH
WEPT
WIFE
WOMAN OF WORTH

```
T O W N W A S S T I R R E D N O L H A M
D H T R O W F O N A M O W M B N A O M I
A U R M E A L T I M E L P O A O R P A H
U S E E L I M E L E C H A A R I A Q N O
G B D E S R U N M R O Z U B L T M S O B
H A E S E H T O L C T S E B E P G T S E
T N E M S V I D Y O N D A E Y E R L E D
E D M I W E E N O X E Z F W H C A A R L
R D I D A S R K G I B S H G A N C D O E
S I M N S C R U D F I T N E R O I N B I
I E G I H U S S S H L I F H V C O A F F
N D K G T G N E D A N O A I E H U S O N
L N J H P O E E E R E D O M S O S T U I
A T K T S A R W O L U M Y R T Q R A N D
W W I F E E F M R J X A X V C S A R D E
E O T H V O E X C H A N G I N G E T F N
P S S O N S T O O K W I V E S U Y L A A
T O C A N O I N T D C H I L I O N E V E
W N M E H E L H T E B F A M I N E D O L
U S E B Z R E H O T G N U L C H T U R G
```

Word Search 20

NOAH AND THE ARK

Why did God pick Noah to build the ark? Find out in Genesis 6-8.

ALTAR

BURNT OFFERINGS

CATTLE

COVENANT

CREEPING THINGS

DOOR

DOVE

FIFTY CUBITS

FLOOD

FOOD

FORTY DAYS AND NIGHTS

FOWLS

GOPHER WOOD

HAM

JAPHETH

LOWER STORY

MOUNTAIN OF ARARAT

OLIVE LEAF

PITCH

RAIN

RAINBOW

RAVEN

ROOMS

SECOND STORY

SHEM

SIDES

SIX HUNDRED YEARS OLD

SONS' WIVES

THIRD STORY

THREE HUNDRED CUBITS

TWO OF EVERY SORT

WIFE

WINDOW

```
F O O D A T Y R O T S D R I H T A D
O E L T T A C B D H F J H C B R L O
R A V E N R R U C R G K T I E O T O
T A K S N A W R S E D I S Y S S A W
Y O I T I R O N L E P Q W R G Y R R
D U P N V A D T J H R S A O N R M E
A X F A B F N O A U D E Z T I E C H
Y B E G D O I F P N Y V W S H V Y P
S M O O R N W F H D H I O R T E K O
A N V J M I L E E R F W L E G F I G
N E R U O A V R T E P S I W N O W S
D O O L F T D I H D Q N V O I O T X
N C O V E N A N T C Y O E L P W A D
I E O Z U U O G D U H S L B E T O S
G J F H M O I S K B N C E L E O G L
H P X Y U M E H S I R C A X R V M W
T I S T I B U C Y T F I F S C A B O
S Z T S E C O N D S T O R Y H W A F
```

Word Search 21

OLD TESTAMENT MEN AND WOMEN
OF GREAT FAITH

These men and women are listed in Hebrews 11:4-40.

ABEL	JEPHTHAH
ABRAHAM	JOSEPH
BARAK	MOSES
DAVID	NOAH
ENOCH	RAHAB
GIDEON	SAMSON
ISAAC	SAMUEL
JACOB	SARAH

BONUS BIBLE TRIVIA

When King Xerxes couldn't sleep, he had people
read the record of his reign to him.   Esther 6:1

A	L	E	U	M	A	S	B	F	A
S	B	I	D	L	K	A	R	A	B
A	A	R	E	N	O	C	H	G	E
R	H	E	A	H	C	A	J	C	L
A	A	K	M	H	H	S	A	D	N
H	R	P	J	T	A	A	N	A	O
N	O	A	H	A	S	M	O	V	E
U	Q	P	S	I	C	S	W	I	D
S	E	S	O	M	T	O	R	D	I
J	O	S	E	P	H	N	B	V	G

Word Search 22

PARABLES OF JESUS

BARREN FIG TREE

DISHONEST STEWARD

FATHER AND TWO SONS

FOUND TREASURE

GOOD SAMARITAN

LABORERS IN VINEYARD

LEAVEN

LOST PIECE OF MONEY

LOST SHEEP

MARRIAGE FEAST

MUSTARD SEED

NET

PHARISEE AND PUBLICAN

POUNDS

PRECIOUS PEARL

PRODIGAL SON

RICH FOOL

RICH MAN AND LAZARUS

SEED

SHEEP AND GOATS

SOWER

TALENTS

TARES

TEN VIRGINS

TWO DEBTORS

UNJUST JUDGE

UNMERCIFUL SERVANT

VINEYARD

WAITING SERVANTS

```
P R E C I O U S P E A R L C F D E E S
F H I L D R I C H F O O L O G S P D I
H T A C J P O U N D S E U K D T R W S
Y M N R H S E R A T S N O E P A O A N
E T E A I M Q N S U D R E N Y O D I O
N W E T V S A H Z T X S B E W G I T S
O O R N U R E N R V D A N V Y D G I O
M D T C V E E E A R F I G A E N A N W
F E G A P I A S A N V D N E S A L G T
O B I H L S R T L N D J E L O P S S D
E T F K U E S G I U D L T I W E O E N
C O N R L U N S I M F P A N E E N R A
E R E P M Q R T R N S I U Z R H O V R
I S R T A E Z C S W S D C B A S X A E
P U R D R A Y E N I V Y B R L R V N H
T E A O U N J U S T J U D G E I U T T
S G B T S A E F E G A I R R A M C S A
O A H F G O O D S A M A R I T A N A F
L D I S H O N E S T S T E W A R D U N
```

D	J	C	O	R	I	N	T	H	I	A	N	S
H	I	O	S	F	Q	M	S	P	K	G	N	N
G	A	L	A	T	I	A	N	S	T	A	E	A
O	T	O	W	N	V	R	A	X	I	U	L	I
B	Y	S	S	H	D	J	M	N	T	F	A	P
I	C	S	K	N	L	E	O	Z	U	M	G	P
Y	N	I	X	R	A	L	R	Y	S	T	P	I
H	S	A	Q	W	A	I	V	O	A	Z	U	L
T	B	N	F	S	I	K	S	O	D	M	H	I
O	J	S	S	E	L	Q	C	E	P	G	N	H
M	R	E	B	X	G	U	F	Y	H	V	A	P
I	H	C	N	O	M	E	L	I	H	P	H	T
T	W	D	S	E	Z	S	W	E	R	B	E	H

Word Search 23

PARTING OF THE RED SEA

Read all about one of the greatest miracles of the Old Testament in Exodus 14.

ANGEL OF GOD

ARMY

CHANGED MIND

CHARIOTS

DEAD UPON SEASHORE

DRY GROUND

EGYPTIANS

ENCAMPED BY SEA

GREAT FEAR

LIFT ROD

MORNING

MOSES

NIGHT PASSED

PEOPLE OF ISRAEL

PHARAOH

PILLAR OF CLOUD

PURSUED

SEA RETURNED

SERVANTS

STRETCH HAND OVER SEA

STRONG EAST WIND

WALL

WATERS DIVIDED

```
D N I W T S A E G N O R T S D M H A
I E W N S Q J V A E Z X K Y R F E E
P H A R A O H G P U L Y T W M S O S
E B T D R Y G R O U N D G D R R I Y
O F E H U C E D O G F O L E G N A B
P J R G R P M Q T V L Y V S X I O D
L N S R Y M O S E S Z O K P U G W E
E A D E G P D N I M D E G N A H C P
O D I A E B T L S N H N C L F T I M
F J V T O R L I A E I L Q I U P N A
I C I F S A K H A N A T P F M A D C
S H D E W V H Y R N E S A T C S E N
R A E A Z C B O F D S W H R X S U E
A R D R T J M U G O B I T O P E S Q
E I D E N R U T E R A E S D R D R H
L O R A L B M C N D O F P G S E U Y
S T N A V R E S V L C S Z X M A P R
S S N W K P I L L A R O F C L O U D
```

Word Search 24

PAULINE LETTERS
(in the order they appear in the Bible)

ROMANS

CORINTHIANS (1&2)

GALATIANS

EPHESIANS

PHILIPPIANS

COLOSSIANS

THESSALONIANS (1&2)

TIMOTHY (1&2)

TITUS

PHILEMON

HEBREWS

BONUS BIBLE TRIVIA

Israelites were forbidden to wear clothes made of
two kinds of material. Leviticus 19:19

Word Search 25

PRODIGAL SON

What did the prodigal son's father do when his son returned home? Find out in Luke 15:11-32.

ANGRY	GATHERED
BEST ROBE	GREAT FAMINE
BROTHER	JOURNEY
COMPASSION	KISSED
DANCING	MUSIC
DIVIDED	NO LONGER WORTHY
EAT AND MAKE MERRY	PODS
ELDER SON	RING
EMBRACED	SHARE OF PROPERTY
FAR COUNTRY	SHOES
FATHER	SINNED
FATTED CALF	SPENT EVERYTHING
FEED SWINE	SQUANDERED
FIELDS	YOUNGER SON

```
E H J O U R N E Y R G N A G S F
G N O L O N G E R W O R T H Y A
N B F D E R E H T A G I O T R T
I R D I B J R O N M Q E R S R H
H O E V C E N L U P S E K D E E
T T R I K O S U O W P D S L M R
Y H E D I T M T C O E V D E E E
R E D E S X A P R C H E E I K N
E R N D S C F P A O R Y N F A I
V B A G E Z F R F S B D N E M W
E I U N D O B K O G S E I U D S
T O Q J E M P N L Q N I S M N D
N O S R E G N U O Y R I O U A E
E D A N C I N G S V C X R N T E
P H Y A T W F L A C D E T T A F
S D O P G R E A T F A M I N E Z
```

Word Search 26

PSALM 23 (RSV)

Locate and loop only the words underlined in this psalm.

"The <u>Lord</u> is my <u>shepherd</u>, I shall not <u>want</u>; he <u>makes</u> me lie down in <u>green</u> <u>pastures</u>.

He <u>leads</u> me <u>beside</u> still <u>waters</u>; he <u>restores</u> my <u>soul</u>.

He leads me in <u>paths</u> of <u>righteousness</u> for his name's <u>sake</u>.

Even though I <u>walk</u> through the <u>valley</u> of the <u>shadow</u> of <u>death</u>, I <u>fear</u> no <u>evil</u>; for thou <u>art</u> with me; thy <u>rod</u> and thy <u>staff</u>, they <u>comfort</u> me.

Thou <u>preparest</u> a <u>table</u> before me in the <u>presence</u> of my <u>enemies</u>; thou <u>anointest</u> my <u>head</u> with <u>oil</u>, my <u>cup</u> <u>overflows</u>.

Surely <u>goodness</u> and <u>mercy</u> shall <u>follow</u> me all the <u>days</u> of my <u>life</u>; and I shall <u>dwell</u> in the <u>house</u> of the Lord <u>for ever</u>."

```
R E S T O R E S E R U T S A P
E F I N L H S E M E R C Y R R
V J S L O R D K M O E K G T E
E D I S E B O A F F Q L L R P
R S E T E N E M I E S G I P A
O D A A T N O L Z X R U O V R
F W V F T C S P R E S E N C E
O E Y F G H W U E W O D A H S
L L A Y O D A N O I N T E S T
L L C E O W A L K E I K B G E
O U F L D H F S J L T A B L E
W O M L N R E S H E P H E R D
A S D A E L A Y E T R P G N D
N O S V S Q R A A S A K E I O
T H O U S E T D D V U P U C R
```

Word Search 27

Locate and loop only the words underlined in this last psalm.

"Praise the Lord!

Praise God in his sanctuary; praise him in his mighty firmament!

Praise him for his mighty deeds; praise him according to his exceeding greatness!

Praise him with trumpet sound; praise him with lute and harp!

Praise him with timbrel and dance; praise him with strings and pipe!

Praise him with sounding cymbals; praise him with loud clashing cymbals!

Let everything that breathes praise the Lord!

Praise the Lord!"

```
E  C  Y  M  B  A  L  S  D  E  E  D
X  V  P  F  H  P  R  A  I  S  E  O
C  L  E  R  B  M  I  T  A  S  M  G
E  I  G  R  A  D  A  N  C  E  I  G
E  T  U  L  Y  H  C  J  L  N  G  N
D  B  R  E  A  T  H  E  S  T  H  I
I  M  L  O  U  D  H  N  K  A  T  D
N  P  D  A  N  O  P  I  P  E  Y  R
G  T  R  U  M  P  E  T  N  R  Q  O
T  Y  O  R  S  T  R  I  N  G  S  C
U  S  L  S  G  N  I  H  S  A  L  C
T  N  E  M  A  M  R  I  F  W  V  A
```

Word Search 28

QUEEN ESTHER

Find out how and why Esther was made queen in Esther 2:1-18.

ASKED FOR NOTHING

BANQUET

BEAUTY

BEST PLACE IN HAREM

CONCUBINES

CROWN

CUSTODY OF HEGAI

EVENING

FAVOR

FOUND GRACE

GIFTS

GIVEN WHAT SHE DESIRED

HADASSAH

JEW

KING AHASUERUS

MADE HER QUEEN

MORDECAI ADOPTED HER

MORNING

NO MOTHER OR FATHER

OIL OF MYRRH

OINTMENTS

PALACE

PLEASED

PORTION OF FOOD

PRINCES

REMISSION OF TAXES

SERVANTS

SEVEN CHOSEN MAIDS

SHAASHGAZ

SPICES

TENTH MONTH

THE KING LOVED ESTHER

TWELVE MONTHS

VIRGIN

```
R E H D E T P O D A I A C E D R O M D
T W E L V E M O N T H S B A N Q U E T
C H K B E S T P L A C E I N H A R E M
G R E I K M I H R R Y M F O L I O N O
A G O K N I G R I V J L H D S E S O R
S N I W I G N I N E V E O E O C E M N
K P N F N N A T Y W U O D P S A C O I
E H T R T V G H X Q F E R L P R I T N
D A M O Z S B L A F H C A E R G P H G
F S E V E N C H O S E N M A I D S E S
O S N A D H Y N T V U J E S N N E R E
R A T F G T O A K I E E F E C U R O N
N D S L U I H W E J M D R D E O V R I
O A N A T W Q P A L A C E U S F A F B
T H E R N Z A G H S A A H S S O N A U
H B O E R H T N O M H T N E T P T T C
I P V N E E U Q R E H E D A M H S H N
N I C U S T O D Y O F H E G A I E E O
G T S E X A T F O N O I S S I M E R C
```

Word Search 29

QUEEN OF SHEBA

Find out what happened when the Queen of Sheba tested King Solomon in 1 Kings 10:1-13.

"BLESSED BE THE LORD"	NO MORE SPIRIT
BURNT OFFERINGS	OFFICIALS
CAMELS	PRECIOUS STONES
CUPBEARERS	QUEEN OF SHEBA
EXPLAIN	REPORT WAS TRUE
FOOD	RIGHTEOUSNESS
GREAT RETINUE	SERVANTS
HARD QUESTIONS	SPICES
HOUSE	TALENTS OF GOLD
JERUSALEM	TEST
JUSTICE	WISDOM
KING SOLOMON	

```
H M J T A L E N T S O F G O L D
N S S E N O T S S U O I C E R P
S S L N K I N G S O L O M O N S
G E K P O Q I O C N I A L P X E
N N Q E C I T S U J R E C W T C
I S U V S Z T X P A H B A U Y I
R U E F C J W S B T H L M K E P
E O E E U N I T E R T A E R G S
F E N G D T S B A U M I L S P L
F T O T N S D Q R W Q U S O E A
O H F R X E O V E Z B D A Y S I
T G S F S T M I R C J E R H U C
N I H S J E R U S A L E M A O I
R R E P O R T W A S T R U E H F
U L B D S T N A V R E S D O O F
B G A N O M O R E S P I R I T O
```

Word Search 30

RAHAB AND THE SPIES

Read all about Rahab's great courage and faith in Joshua 2:1-22.

BLOOD	MEN WENT OUT
CLOSED	NO COURAGE LEFT
DARK	OATH
DEALT KINDLY	"OUR LIFE FOR YOURS"
DELIVER FROM DEATH	PURSUED
FORDS	RAHAB
GATE	RESPECT
GUILTLESS	ROOF
HARLOT	ROPE
HEARTS MELTED	SAVE FAMILY
HIDE THREE DAYS	SCARLET CORD
HILLS	SPIES
HOUSE	STALKS OF FLAX
JERICHO	STREET
JORDAN	SURE SIGN
JOSHUA	TWO MEN
KING	WINDOW
LODGED	

```
O H C I R E J O S H U A I M K H
S U N O C O U R A G E L E F T I
J D R O C T E L R A C S M A L D
H A R L O T N P U R S U E D X E
H E D O I T W O M E N D N O A T
E S E W F F E P L R M O W O L H
A U A Q I T E T K O U S E L F R
R O L V A N L F R R T N N B F E
T H T G E I D F O C A A T N O E
S T K V U F R O L R X D O G S D
M C I G W E A O W O Y R U I K A
E E N N V B S M Y P A O T S L Y
L P D I Z E S P I E S J U E A S
T S L K D E G D O L T E E R T S
E E Y R A H A B C F Y H G U S E
D R O O F H T A O H I L L S I D
```

Word Search 31

SADDEST VERSE IN THE BIBLE

Locate and loop only the words underlined in this verse found in Mark 15:34 (KJV).

"And at the <u>ninth</u> <u>hour</u> <u>Jesus</u> <u>cried</u> with a <u>loud</u> <u>voice</u>, <u>saying</u>, <u>Eloi</u>, Eloi, <u>lama</u> <u>sabachthani</u>? <u>which is</u>, being <u>interpreted</u>, <u>My God</u>, my God, <u>why</u> hast thou <u>forsaken</u> me?"

BONUS BIBLE TRIVIA

There were 12 baskets full of leftovers when Jesus fed a crowd of people. Matthew 14:20

```
H  T  N  I  N  J  M  E  L  O  I
K  O  F  O  R  S  A  K  E  N  N
S  N  U  T  D  J  R  O  A  L  T
Q  V  Z  R  E  P  A  H  U  Y  E
W  B  X  S  I  E  T  I  C  W  R
H  F  U  E  R  H  G  W  H  D  P
I  S  P  M  C  S  M  H  Q  J  R
C  A  M  A  L  I  K  Y  T  O  E
H  N  B  L  R  U  O  Z  G  V  T
I  A  C  W  D  Y  A  V  X  O  E
S  A  Y  I  N  G  B  L  O  U  D
```

Word Search 32

SAMSON AND DELILAH

What happened to Samson when Delilah had his head shaved? Read all about it in Judges 14-16.

ASHKELON	LION	TORCHES
AVENGED	OLIVE ORCHARDS	TORMENT
BIND	PILLARS	WATER
BOWSTRINGS	PRISON	WEAK
BRONZE FETTERS	RAID	WEAVE
BURIED	RAZOR	WEB
BURNED	RIDDLE	WEPT
DAUGHTER OF PHILISTINE	ROCK OF ETAM	WIFE
DEATH	ROPES	
DELILAH	SAMSON	
ENTICE	SECRET	
FEAST	SEVEN DAYS	
FESTAL GARMENTS	SEVEN LOCKS	
FOXES	SEVENTH DAY	
GAZA	SHAVED	
GAZITES	SILVER	
GRAIN	SLAUGHTER	
HARLOT	SMOTE	
HOLLOW PLACES	SPLIT	
HONEY	STRENGTH	
HOT ANGER	SWARM OF BEES	
JAWBONE	THIRSTY	
KILLED	THIRTY COMPANIONS	
LEHI	TIMNAH	
LINEN GARMENTS	TOMB OF MANOAH	

```
T O M B O F M A N O A H A D R I D D L E
S H L B C S G N I R T S W O B G A Z N H
A O I U E F B S D R A H C R O E V I L O
E T N R D E L I L A H Q O D E A T H Y L
F A E I T H Y A D H T N E V E S S W T L
S N N E O Y E N O H Z I P L I N I K S O
T G G D R J C O S E P O R L M F L E R W
N E A I M A B O F L E H I D E R V N I P
E R R A E I Z E M R I H S E E E E O H L
M E M R N B T O S P P O O L N T R B T A
R T E D T T U R R F A T N L T H D W G C
A A N S E H C R O T U N O I I G E A A E
G W T R V K X R N C P C I K C U G J Z S
L A S H A V E D Z E K E W O E A N W I E
A T Z E J T I L P S D O W E N L E E T T
T I W A H T G N E R T S F L I S V B E O
S M K G R A I N G B S E V E N D A Y S M
E N U P I L L A R S E X O F T E R C E S
F A E V A E W S E E B F O M R A W S C H
D H A R L O T D N O L E K H S A M S O N
```

Word Search 33

SHORTEST CHAPTER IN THE BIBLE

Locate and loop only the words underlined in this 117th psalm (KJV).

"O <u>praise</u> the <u>Lord</u>, all ye <u>nations</u>: praise him, all ye <u>people</u>.

For his <u>merciful</u> <u>kindness</u> is <u>great</u> <u>toward</u> us: and the <u>truth</u> of the Lord <u>endureth</u> for ever. Praise ye the Lord."

BONUS BIBLE TRIVIA

David pretended to be insane once by marking up a door and drooling all over his face. 1 Samuel 21:13

```
E   S   I   A   R   P   K   L   N
D   N   O   L   E   S   U   Q   K
R   P   D   O   M   F   R   T   I
O   T   P   U   I   X   O   T   N
L   L   U   C   R   W   V   R   D
E   W   R   B   A   E   Y   U   N
Z   E   G   R   E   A   T   T   E
M   C   D   H   A   G   E   H   S
D   F   N   A   T   I   O   N   S
```

Word Search 34

SOLOMON'S PRAYER OF DEDICATION

Locate and loop only the words underlined in these verses found in 2 Chronicles 6:41-42 (RSV).

"And now <u>arise</u>, O Lord God, and go to thy <u>resting</u> <u>place</u>, thou and the <u>ark</u> of thy <u>might</u>.

Let thy <u>priests</u>, O Lord God, be <u>clothed</u> with <u>salvation</u>, and let thy <u>saints</u> <u>rejoice</u> in thy <u>goodness</u>.

O Lord God, do not <u>turn</u> <u>away</u> the <u>face</u> of thy <u>anointed</u> one!

<u>Remember</u> thy <u>steadfast</u> <u>love</u> for <u>David</u> thy <u>servant</u>."

BONUS BIBLE TRIVIA

When Asa, King of Judah, was old he got diseased feet. 1 Kings 15:23

R	E	M	E	M	B	E	R	L	O	Y
M	P	D	I	V	A	D	M	K	R	A
T	S	D	E	T	N	I	O	N	A	W
S	E	R	E	Q	G	N	O	E	E	A
A	R	S	W	H	U	I	N	C	F	P
F	V	E	T	V	T	R	I	A	T	R
D	A	V	S	A	U	O	C	L	A	I
A	N	O	V	T	J	E	L	P	R	E
E	T	L	X	E	I	B	A	C	I	S
T	A	Z	R	S	T	N	I	A	S	T
S	S	E	N	D	O	O	G	D	E	S

Word Search 35

SON OF THE SHUNAMMITE

Find out what happened when Elisha met a wealthy Shunammite woman in 2 Kings 4:8-37.

BED	LAP
BITTER DISTRESS	LAY STAFF UPON CHILD
BORE SON	MOUNT CARMEL
CHAIR	"MY HEAD, MY HEAD!"
CHILD GREW	OPENED EYES
COMMANDER OF ARMY	PRAYED
CONCEIVED	ROOF CHAMBER
EAT SOME FOOD	SADDLED THE ASS
ELISHA	SERVANT
FEET	SHE HAD NO SON
FLESH BECAME WARM	SHUNEM
GEHAZI	SNEEZED SEVEN TIMES
HE DIED	SPRING
HOLY MAN	STOOD IN DOORWAY
HUSBAND IS OLD	TABLE
KING	WEALTHY WOMAN
LAMP	WORD SPOKEN ON BEHALF

```
L A M P N M Y H E A D M Y H E A D F
S A D D L E D T H E A S S R O N L L
S N Y P S B E D E I D E H O S A O E
E T E S F E E T Z V Q X T P H M S S
R A L E T P R A Y E D M U E E O I H
T B E W Z A H S I L E E B N H W D B
S L M A E E F W B N Y N R E A Y N E
I E R C G R D F O Z O U I D D H A C
D A A K I N G S U N D H A E N T B A
R T C L E I E D E P G S H Y O L S M
E S T A H R F K L V O N C E S A U E
T O N P O J O N L I E N A S O E H W
T M U B S P R I N G H N C M N W K A
I E O M S E R V A N T C T H Y R O R
B F M D E V I E C N O C P I I L Q M
S O R O O F C H A M B E R U M L O T
C O M M A N D E R O F A R M Y E D H
W D V Y A W R O O D N I D O O T S W
```

Word Search 36

TEN COMMANDMENTS

Locate and loop only the words underlined in these commandments found in Exodus 20:3-17 (KJV).

"Thou shalt have no other gods before me."

"Thou shalt not make unto thee any graven image."

"Thou shalt not take the name of the Lord thy God in vain."

"Remember the sabbath day, to keep it holy."

"Honour thy father and thy mother."

"Thou shalt not kill."

"Thou shalt not commit adultery."

"Thou shalt not steal."

"Thou shalt not bear false witness against thy neighbor."

"Thou shalt not covet."

BONUS BIBLE TRIVIA

Nazareth to Bethlehem is approximately 70 miles as the crow flies. As the donkey trots, it's about a three day trip.

```
S  A  B  B  A  T  H  O  N  O  U  R
S  F  E  T  O  G  O  D  S  Q  E  O
E  A  A  P  E  T  A  K  E  M  S  B
N  T  R  T  H  V  W  I  E  R  L  H
T  H  R  E  H  T  O  M  N  O  A  G
I  E  R  O  F  E  B  C  R  S  F  I
W  R  M  A  K  E  N  D  L  H  T  E
S  V  H  Y  R  E  T  L  U  D  A  N
B  X  G  O  V  D  I  A  P  Y  I  A
S  T  E  A  L  K  L  E  F  A  Y  M
C  H  R  J  E  Y  E  Z  V  D  F  E
E  G  A  M  I  K  T  I  M  M  O  C
```

Word Search 37

TEN PLAGUES
(in the order they appear in Exodus 7-12)

BLOOD

FROGS

GNATS

FLIES

(plague) ON CATTLE

BOILS

HAIL

LOCUSTS

DARKNESS

DEATH

BONUS BIBLE TRIVIA

Herod was struck down by God, and his body
was eaten by worms. Acts 12:21-23

```
O    L    O    C    U    S    T    S

P    N    F    R    O    G    S    E

S    W    C    U    N    E    Q    I

B    X    T    A    N    R    B    L

L    U    T    K    T    V    O    F

O    S    R    A    E    T    I    Z

O    A    B    H    A    I    L    C

D    E    A    T    H    D    S    E
```

Word Search 38

TOWER OF BABEL

Why did the people in the land of Shinar want to build a tower with its top in the heavens? Find out in Genesis 11:1-9.

BABEL	LAND OF SHINAR
BEGINNING	MEN MIGRATED
BITUMEN	NOT UNDERSTAND
BRICKS	ONE LANGUAGE
BUILD	ONE PEOPLE
BURN	SCATTERED ABROAD
CITY	SETTLED
CONFUSE	SPEECH
FEW WORDS	THE LORD
FOUND A PLAIN	TOP IN THE HEAVENS
FROM THE EAST	TOWER

```
S C O T M E N M I G R A T E D
K N N F H D J S K C I R B A N
I G E N L E O D P E B M O H A
E T P V P Y L R X D A R S E T
G B E Q A I U O B C B A W C S
A E O F U E V W R A E R Z O R
U G P B H J H W D D L I G N E
G I L T S A E E H T M O R F D
N N E K O E R F H C Y R N U N
A N R U B E T M P T E Q L S U
L I S U T O W T I Y N E B E T
E N X T W C Z C L D T I P V O
N G A E B I T U M E N A P S N
O C R F N I A L P A D N U O F
S L A N D O F S H I N A R E T
```

Word Search 39

TO WHOM DOES GOD GIVE GRACE?

Locate and loop only the words underlined in this verse found in James 4:6 (KJV).

"But he <u>giveth</u> <u>more</u> <u>grace</u>. <u>Wherefore</u> he <u>saith</u>, God <u>resisteth</u> the <u>proud</u>, but giveth grace <u>unto</u> the <u>humble</u>."

BONUS BIBLE TRIVIA

God made the shadow on a sundial go back ten steps as a sign to Hezekiah. 2 Kings 20:11

R	E	S	I	S	T	E	T	H
Q	R	C	X	T	Z	V	T	U
U	O	Y	A	D	W	E	R	M
A	F	D	U	R	V	S	D	B
G	E	O	E	I	G	B	F	L
C	R	G	G	U	N	T	O	E
P	E	N	Q	H	U	K	R	S
L	H	T	I	A	S	O	I	O
R	W	J	P	W	M	V	T	M

Word Search 40

TRANSFIGURATION

Find out what happened when Jesus took Peter, James, and John up a high mountain in Matthew 17:1-8.

APPEARED	JOHN
BELOVED SON	JOHN THE BAPTIST
BRIGHT CLOUD	MOSES
DISCIPLES	PETER
ELIAS	RAIMENT WAS WHITE
FACE DID SHINE	SORE AFRAID
"HEAR YE HIM"	THREE TABERNACLES
HIGH MOUNTAIN	TRANSFIGURED
JAMES	UNDERSTOOD
JESUS	VOICE

BONUS BIBLE TRIVIA

The Gospel of Luke was written to Theophilus.
Luke 1:3

R E T E P B E R C Y I U W S F S

V A P P E A R E D W Z S E E E O

B R I G H T C L O U D U L L N R

A E D M X V O I C E N T C P I E

D J L G E S K A M D H A P I H A

E L V O E N O S E O N R L C S F

R W S M V U T R M R S N E S D R

U P A Y T E S W E X Q E A I I A

G J E Z J T D B A N B G S D D I

I F N H O J A S H S L A E O E D

F C K O P T M U O D W I D Q C R

S X D X E S C S V N E H A U A D

N T H E A R Y E H I M B I W F Y

A M R Q F T N J U I S O J T R K

R H I G H M O U N T A I N G E P

T S I T P A B E H T N H O J H L

Word Search 41

TWELVE DISCIPLES

ANDREW

BARTHOLOMEW

JAMES (son of Alphaeus)

JAMES (son of Zebedee)

JOHN

JUDAS

MATTHEW

PETER

PHILIP

SIMON

THADDAEUS

THOMAS

BONUS BIBLE TRIVIA

When Nebuchadnezzar went insane, he grew claws like a bird and hair like an eagle's feathers, and ate grass like a cow. Daniel 4:33

B	Z	S	I	M	O	N	A	S	T	V
W	A	T	A	P	I	L	I	H	P	S
G	X	R	B	D	F	U	A	C	E	Y
D	T	J	T	H	U	D	E	M	T	I
N	H	T	K	H	D	J	A	P	E	M
U	O	O	S	A	O	J	Q	L	R	A
S	M	Y	E	V	M	L	D	A	R	T
Z	A	U	M	X	C	E	O	W	B	T
P	S	F	A	M	U	I	S	M	O	H
J	T	Q	J	O	H	N	K	G	E	E
N	V	H	R	L	A	N	D	R	E	W

Word Search 42

WEDDING AT CANA

Read all about Jesus' first miracle in John 2:1-11.

BRIDEGROOM

BRIM

CANA OF GALILEE

DISCIPLES

FIRKINS

GLORY

JESUS CALLED

MANIFESTED FORTH

MARRIAGE

MIRACLE

MOTHER OF JESUS

RULER OF THE FEAST

SERVANTS

SIX WATERPOTS

TASTED

WATER

WINE

BONUS BIBLE TRIVIA

Samson killed more people when he died than he did when he lived. Judges 16:30

```
R  E  T  A  W  E  T  L  A  J  W  G  Y  C  H
F  U  Y  B  M  I  R  A  C  L  E  D  B  T  U
D  E  L  L  A  C  S  U  S  E  J  V  R  S  Z
I  K  S  E  R  V  A  N  T  S  I  O  I  I  H
S  I  P  B  R  U  K  F  M  X  F  R  D  X  E
C  V  Q  Z  I  O  N  G  C  D  M  Y  E  W  S
I  F  A  J  A  H  F  T  E  W  I  O  G  A  D
P  S  I  F  G  Y  P  T  E  A  R  V  R  T  W
L  B  T  R  E  J  S  Q  H  X  B  H  O  E  C
E  G  Y  U  K  E  Z  D  I  E  K  R  O  R  D
S  M  E  R  F  I  K  A  N  I  F  C  M  P  E
F  O  J  I  O  P  N  I  H  L  N  E  G  O  T
D  B  N  Q  M  L  W  S  B  N  C  S  A  T  S
C  A  N  A  O  F  G  A  L  I  L  E  E  S  A
M  O  T  H  E  R  O  F  J  E  S  U  S  R  T
```

Word Search 43

WHAT IS FAITH?

Locate and loop only the words underlined in these verses found in Hebrews 11:1-3 (KJV).

"Now <u>faith</u> is the <u>substance</u> of <u>things</u> <u>hoped</u> for, the <u>evidence</u> of things <u>not seen</u>.

For by it the <u>elders</u> <u>obtained</u> a <u>good</u> <u>report</u>.

Through faith we <u>understand</u> that the <u>worlds</u> were <u>framed</u> by the <u>word of God</u>, so that things which are seen were not <u>made</u> of things which do <u>appear</u>."

BONUS BIBLE TRIVIA

Noah's ark had three stories. Genesis 6:16

S	W	E	V	I	D	E	N	C	E	R
R	T	O	R	A	E	P	P	A	D	V
E	H	B	R	Y	W	D	S	N	U	E
D	O	T	Z	D	O	X	A	S	F	C
L	P	A	I	O	O	T	B	D	R	N
E	E	I	G	A	S	F	C	L	A	A
A	D	N	E	R	F	D	G	R	M	T
H	N	E	E	S	T	O	N	O	E	S
M	A	D	E	L	N	F	I	W	D	B
G	N	T	R	O	P	E	R	O	J	U
U	M	Q	K	P	T	H	I	N	G	S

Word Search 44

WHAT IS LOVE?

Read all about it in 1 Corinthians 13.

(not) ARROGANT

BEARS (all things)

BELIEVES (all things)

(not) BOASTFUL

ENDURES (all things)

HOPES (all things)

(does not) INSIST (on its own way)

(not) IRRITABLE

(not) JEALOUS

KIND

NEVER (ends)

PATIENT

(does not) REJOICE (at wrong)

(not) RESENTFUL

(rejoices in the) RIGHT

(not) RUDE

```
I  A  R  R  O  G  A  N  T  R  A
B  R  S  E  R  U  D  N  E  P  C
J  B  R  D  E  R  F  S  H  A  G
H  E  I  I  I  J  E  E  O  T  K
L  A  A  M  T  N  N  V  P  I  E
O  R  P  L  T  A  S  E  E  E  C
Q  S  U  F  O  R  B  I  S  N  I
R  T  U  D  U  U  V  L  S  T  O
W  L  X  Y  E  Z  S  E  E  T  J
L  U  F  T  S  A  O  B  A  B  E
K  I  N  D  C  D  T  H  G  I  R
```

Word Search 45

WHAT SHALL WE DO TO INHERIT
ETERNAL LIFE?

Locate and loop only the words underlined in this verse
found in Luke 10:27 (RSV).

"You shall love the Lord your God with all your heart,
and with all your soul, and with all your strength, and
with all your mind; and your neighbor as yourself."

BONUS BIBLE TRIVIA

The Holy Place in the Tabernacle contained three
things—the lampstand, the wood table, and the
consecrated bread. Hebrews 9:2

H	T	G	N	E	R	T	S
M	E	S	F	B	I	H	X
I	E	A	C	Y	A	J	T
N	V	U	R	L	O	R	D
D	O	Z	L	T	U	D	V
F	L	E	S	R	U	O	Y
H	A	W	G	O	D	E	S
N	E	I	G	H	B	O	R

Word Search 46

WHY DO WE SOMETIMES FAIL TO RECEIVE
WHEN WE ASK?

Locate and loop only the words underlined in this verse
found in James 4:3 (KJV).

"Ye ask, and receive not, because ye ask amiss, that ye
may consume it upon your lusts."

BONUS BIBLE TRIVIA

An ebenezer is a memorial stone. 1 Samuel 7:12

```
C  O  N  S  U  M  E  T
X  F  E  H  U  A  E  C
L  U  S  T  S  V  Y  V
Z  P  U  S  I  W  B  Y
Y  O  A  E  I  D  A  N
O  N  C  L  E  M  G  O
U  E  E  I  T  H  A  T
R  J  B  M  K  A  S  K
```

Word Search 47

WIDOW'S OIL

Find out how the widow was able to pay her debts in 2 Kings 4:1-7.

BORROW VESSELS	PAY DEBTS
CREDITOR	POUR
CRIED TO ELISHA	SELL
FEAR THE LORD	SHUT THE DOOR
HOUSE	SLAVES
HUSBAND IS DEAD	STOPPED FLOWING
JAR OF OIL	TWO CHILDREN
MAIDSERVANT	WIFE

BONUS BIBLE TRIVIA

Seraphim (the plural of seraph) are the angel-type beings Isaiah saw. Isaiah 6

```
G V T N A V R E S D I A M H
E N I W C Z H W R G D B A U
A D I H O U S E U R F H X S
R P L W Y C S U O J S M T B
O T I N O K H L P I Q B V A
T X O S W L E I L O E R L N
I E F Y L H F E L D A W C D
D B O D T A O D Y D F I Z I
E K R R P T V A E S R F O S
R T A Y D V P E R P X E L D
C E J E Q M Z W S N P U N E
F E I G A S E L L F D O B A
C R O O D E H T T U H S T D
C B O R R O W V E S S E L S
```

Word Search 48

WOMAN AT THE WELL

Find out what Jesus said to the woman at Jacob's well in John 4:1-26.

DEPARTED	MESSIAH
DRAW WATER	NEVER THIRST AGAIN
DRINK	NO DEALINGS
ETERNAL LIFE	PASS THROUGH
FIVE HUSBANDS	SAMARIA
GALILEE	SIXTH HOUR
JACOB'S WELL	SYCHAR
JESUS	TESTIMONY
JEW	WEARY
LEFT JUDEA	WENT AWAY TO CITY
LEFT WATER JAR	WOMAN
LIVING WATER	

```
W R U C I K Y E A G W E A R Y N
L E F T W A T E R J A R V J I O
I T N E H G U O R H T S S A P D
V A Z T D J D F D A W B G C H E
I W I E A R L X E I O A A O S A
N W T R I W P V P S T M L B R L
G A W N A Q A N A S U X I S Y I
W R K A V M S Y R E Z B L W D N
A D W L Y C A I T M A T E E X G
T Q E L U K H S E O S H E L N S
E L R I W T U F D S C U I L O V
R M G F R U O H H T X I S J P T
F I V E H U S B A N D S T E T J
X D V U A T E S T I M O N Y J E
L E F T J U D E A Y E V I B G W
N A M O W F W C H Z S Y C H A R
```

Word Search 49

WOMEN OF THE BIBLE

ABIGAIL	LEAH
AHINOAM	MARTHA
BATHSHEBA	MARY
BILHAH	MARY MAGDALENE
DAMARIS	MIRIAM
DEBORAH	NAOMI
DELILAH	QUEEN OF SHEBA
DINAH	QUEEN VASHTI
DORCAS	RACHEL
ELIZABETH	RAHAB
ESTHER	REBEKAH
EVE	RUTH
HAGAR	SALOME
HANNAH	SARAH
JEZEBEL	ZILPAH
JUDITH	ZIPPORAH

M	A	O	N	I	H	A	E	J	E	Z	E	B	E	L
D	A	M	A	R	I	S	S	A	C	R	O	D	V	E
E	S	R	A	G	A	H	T	J	X	D	I	N	A	H
B	A	Z	Y	B	A	T	H	S	H	E	B	A	L	C
O	R	V	R	M	T	P	E	B	L	N	B	B	D	A
R	A	E	O	A	A	D	R	I	S	I	Q	E	U	R
A	H	V	J	R	F	G	Z	W	G	Y	L	H	E	A
H	T	E	U	Y	C	A	D	A	H	I	A	S	H	N
A	R	B	D	I	B	D	I	A	L	P	Z	F	A	R
R	A	G	I	E	I	L	T	A	L	E	L	O	N	E
O	M	V	T	X	L	E	H	I	M	E	M	N	N	B
P	R	H	H	P	H	C	Z	O	A	I	N	E	A	E
P	M	I	R	I	A	M	L	H	O	A	U	E	H	K
I	Q	S	R	A	H	A	B	M	Y	H	T	U	R	A
Z	K	I	T	H	S	A	V	N	E	E	U	Q	W	H

Word Search 50

ZACCHAEUS

Find out why Zacchaeus climbed the sycamore tree in Luke 19:1-10.

CROWD

GIVE TO THE POOR

GUEST

HALF OF GOODS

HOUSE

JERICHO

JESUS

RESTORE FOURFOLD

RICH

SALVATION

SINNER

SMALL OF STATURE

SYCAMORE TREE

TAX COLLECTOR

ZACCHAEUS

BONUS BIBLE TRIVIA

Jacob made the coat that he gave to Joseph, his favorite son. Genesis 37:3

```
Z N F Z A C C H A E U S L R D
H S D O O G F O F L A H P L B
G T M D B F J H X L V J O D Z
I N V A Z D L J V T X F H B S
V Q Y R L A S A U W R F P I Y
E M D E I L T C H U G O N K C
T E W J U I O G O S Y N B Q A
O C O W O A H F U X E D F Z M
T H R N P T E I S R N J R V O
H F C L D R B H E T S E U G R
E C R I O G X I T U A V E Z E
P W O T R S K Y S U Q T A I T
O A S E Y E C E O M K Q U W R
O E G M S U J C E I H C I R E
R O T C E L L O C X A T G A E
```

Puzzle #1

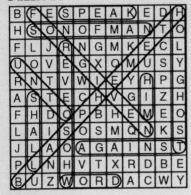

Puzzle #2

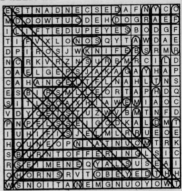

Puzzle #3

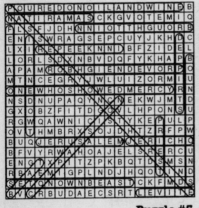

Puzzle #4

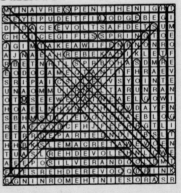

Puzzle #5

Puzzle #6

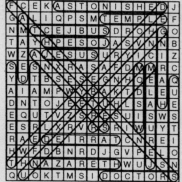

Puzzle #7

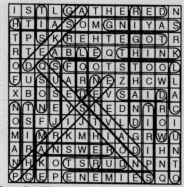

Puzzle #8

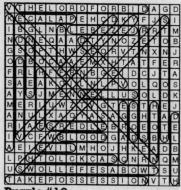

Puzzle #9

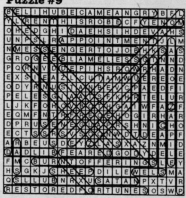

Puzzle #10

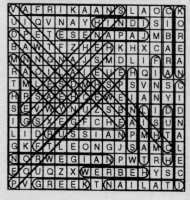

Puzzle #11

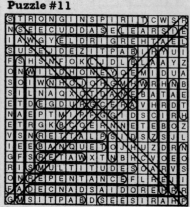

Puzzle #12

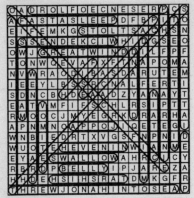

Puzzle #13

Puzzle #14

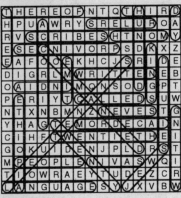

Puzzle #15

Puzzle #16

Puzzle #17

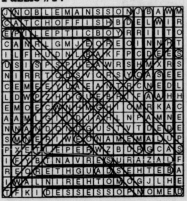

106

Puzzle #18

Puzzle #19

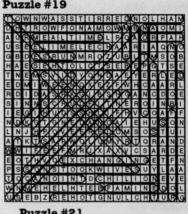

Puzzle #20

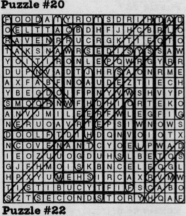

Puzzle #21

Puzzle #22

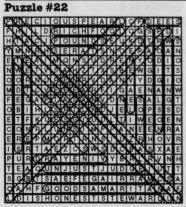

Puzzle #23

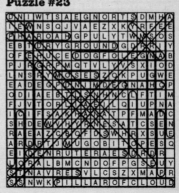

Puzzle #24

Puzzle #25

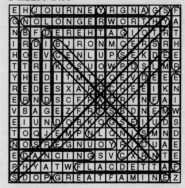

Puzzle #26

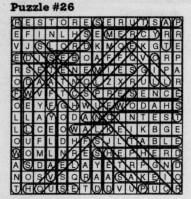

Puzzle #27

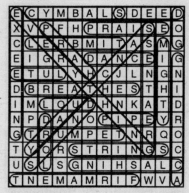

Puzzle #28

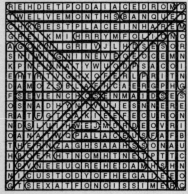

Puzzle #29

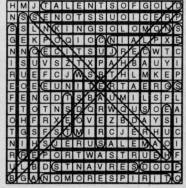

Puzzle #30

Puzzle #31

Puzzle #32

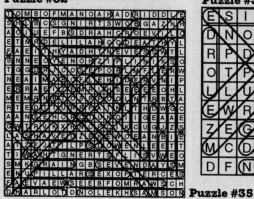

Puzzle #33

Puzzle #34

Puzzle #35

Puzzle #36

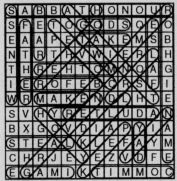

Puzzle #37

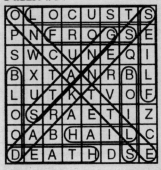

Puzzle #38

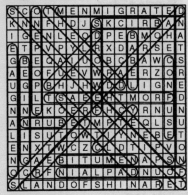

Puzzle #39

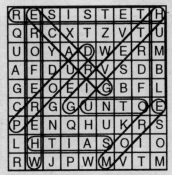

Puzzle #40

Puzzle #41

Puzzle #42

Puzzle #43

Puzzle #44

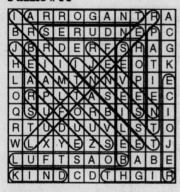

Puzzle #45

Puzzle #46

Puzzle #47

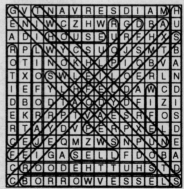

Puzzle #48

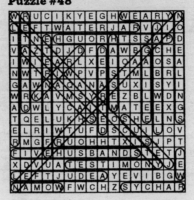

Puzzle #49

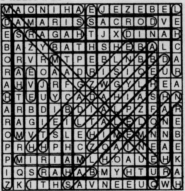

Puzzle #50

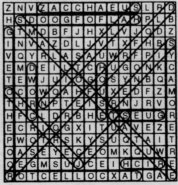

112